Open House

David Brooks spent his earliest years in Greece and Yugoslavia, where his father was an Australian immigration officer. He studied at the Australian National University before completing postgraduate degrees at the University of Toronto, where he was overseas editor for *New Poetry* and worked with such poets as Galway Kinnell, Mark Strand, and Czesław Miłosz. Author of four previous collections of poetry, three of short fiction, four highly acclaimed novels, and a major work of Australian literary history (*The Sons of Clovis*, UQP 2011), his *The Book of Sei* (1985) was heralded as the most impressive debut in Australian short fiction since Peter Carey's, and his second novel, *The Fern Tattoo* (UQP 2007), was short-listed for the Miles Franklin award. The *Sydney Morning Herald* called his previous collection of poetry, *The Balcony* (UQP 2008), 'an electric performance'. Until 2013 he taught Australian Literature at the University of Sydney, where he was also the foundation director of the graduate writing program. Also a renowned editor (of A.D. Hope, R.F. Brissenden) and translator, he is currently co-editor of *Southerly*, lives in the Blue Mountains of New South Wales, and spends a small portion of each year in a village on the coast of Slovenia.

ALSO BY DAVID BROOKS

NOVELS
The House of Balthus
The Fern Tattoo
The Umbrella Club
The Conversation

SHORT FICTION
The Book of Sei and Other Stories
Sheep and the Diva
Black Sea

POETRY
The Cold Front
Walking to Point Clear
Urban Elegies
The Balcony

NON-FICTION
The Necessary Jungle: Literature and excess
De/scription: A Balthus notebook
*The Sons of Clovis: Ern Malley, Adoré Floupette,
and a secret history of Australian poetry*

TRANSLATION
*The Golden Boat: Selected poems of Srečko Kosovel
(with Bert Pribac)*

David Brooks
Open House

UQP

First published 2015 by University of Queensland Press
PO Box 6042, St Lucia, Queensland 4067 Australia

uqp.com.au
uqp@uqp.uq.edu.au

© David Brooks 2015

This book is copyright. Except for private study, research, criticism or
reviews, as permitted under the Copyright Act, no part of this book may be
reproduced, stored in a retrieval system, or transmitted in any form or by
any means without prior written permission. Enquiries should be made to
the publisher.

Cover design/illustration by Sandy Cull, gogoGingko
Typeset in 11.5/14 Adobe Garamond by Post Pre-press Group, Brisbane
Printed in Australia by McPherson's Printing Group, Melbourne

Australian Government

This project has been assisted by the Australian Government
through the Australia Council, its arts funding and advisory body.

Cataloguing-in-Publication Data
National Library of Australia
Cataloguing-in-publication data is available at http://catalogue.nla.gov.au

ISBN 978 0 7022 5352 2 (pbk)
ISBN 978 0 7022 5491 8 (pdf)
ISBN 978 0 7022 5492 5 (epub)
ISBN 978 0 7022 5493 2 (kindle)

University of Queensland Press uses papers that are natural, renewable
and recyclable products made from wood grown in sustainable forests.
The logging and manufacturing processes conform to the environmental
regulations of the country of origin.

to J.S. Harry

Contents

Open House

Report from Blue Mountains

Reading to the Sheep

A Place on Earth

A Place on Earth

A young boy
is sitting by a fire
on the edge of the desert. There's a car
through the scrub behind him
pulled off to the side of the long dirt road
and a tent close by with his father in it, sleeping
already. It is late evening, nine or ten,
and he's long ago eaten: toast, baked
beans on a tin plate, burnt potatoes, tea.
1964 perhaps, or '63:
it doesn't matter what year.
He is sitting by the fire, stoked
earlier so that now it's burned back to the ancient
fire-gutted log he found and dragged there
before the sun set – burned back
so that, now the log is deep alight,
he can see a world in it: sees falling towers, forgotten
Alexandrias and Babylons,
the night markets of Wúzhōu, Rangoon, Hong Kong,
sees Siegfried and the *Götterdämmerung*,
sees a huge, blood-orange sun
setting over the burnt, black
hills around him,
autos-da-fé, charred ruins, faces
staring from the flame
so beautiful they seem to scorch him,
sees the bombing and the burning of Dresden,
bodies in fiery graves, wild
midnight *carnevales*, sees

Moon-men and Sun-men in corroboree,
sees hearth-fires and bonfires and beacon-fires,
Etnas in their scoriac flows,
townspeople and villagers fleeing,
docks and homes and factories alight,
sees battered galleons, masts
collapsing, armadas blazing on the sea, radiant
sunrise breaking from the glowing embers
as if out of a phoenix nest.

Something
rustles in the ti-tree, a
wallaby perhaps, night bird or
wild dog drawn by the fire,
and he looks up from his dreaming, sees the huge
darkness of the night and the vast
canopy of unknown, unnameable stars,
a night so infinite, this night,
it will never leave him.
Time and again he will look up
– for sixty or for seventy years, luck holding – and it
will always be there: before him
the fire, behind him
his father sleeping, that something
rustling in the undergrowth,
and about him the galaxies turning, the still
point of his being,
a place on earth,
gift beyond measure.

The Thick of It

I was standing there, washing up and
thinking about Baudelaire, how one might
give one's soul
to be able to write so well
but then the dog came down
to lap at his water-bowl and
sleep on the armchair
and on some obscure
impulse I went out
into the night air, for the
thick of it, the
hum of life everywhere – looked
at the stars, the
insects
swarming about the back-door lamp, and
coming in, stepped over first a
cockroach then a
slug, leading its
small family somewhere.

How can we
be so arrogant, to think that our
souls are worth so much?

Poem

Since I have come upstairs
on all fours to greet him, the dog,
for such is his wont,
licks first the top of my head and then my left ear, just as,
if he can catch me, he'll
lick any cracked or wounded skin as I
get up in the morning – it's
nothing that I can't wash off
and probably helps
heal some other, more ancient hurt, or
balms it.

It is
a warm spring day. The smell
of each of us
rises gently into the ether, yours
of lemons and woodsmoke, summer flowers, his
of grass and dust and beloved
blanket, mine – for such
is my own
ancient wont –
of you.

Rats, Lice and History[i]

This morning, making coffee, I watched
through the kitchen window an old crow
settle on a low branch of a Blue Mountains Ash and,
looking out over the valley, for no
apparent reason, burst into raucous song,
and I thought – I don't know why – of that other
late summer, so long ago, when,
full of my mother's death
I set out with five hundred new-
earned dollars and a haversack
heavy with volumes of Jack Kerouac
and took flight for the northern winter, to visit
school friends of two years before – landing
in San Francisco, heading for Sacramento
to see the best of them, my namesake, then
betraying him, only five days later, when,
at her invitation, I went to visit his
girlfriend, two hundred miles south
and left sex-sore and sleepless the next morning
by Greyhound for Iowa and the parents
of the first girl I had ever made love with, whose
doctor-father (she was at school elsewhere) regaled me
all evening with *Rats, Lice and History* before
(in such perfect irony) I woke itchy and sore
in his attic guest-bed with new-
hatched Australian crab-lice of my own
and, confessing, was shown the door
with stony silence and a prescription for DDT, his own
attempt, I think, to kill me, though I went on, still

burning, physically, to see
and be rebuffed by his daughter in Milwaukee
and so hastened home to my once-
host-family in Chicago, for three days of rest
before heading for Rochester and the photographs
of Weston and Cameron and Minor White
and a once-dreamt-of night
with Miss Teenage Chicago of four years before,
who sent me, then, to stay with her cousin in Baltimore
who, undeterred by the thought
of her heart-surgeon husband,
would wake me each morning with languid
strokings on the floor – even her name now
lost in the subsequent embarrassment of my telephone call
from a clinic, in St John, Newfoundland, run
by sadists of some Christian order
who had burned and scalded and punctured me,
to tell her of what was almost certainly (but
wasn't) a cousin-to-cousin STD, and then – my true
goal all along – after another five days' travelling,
to S., in Michigan, ten years older than I, who had once, in
    Sydney,
held me so long and so gently, seeing
something I had not yet seen in me,
and we made love at last,
fumbling and sad, in the bleak snow-light,
while her army husband was out,
and she came, and sobbed, and since no-one
had ever come with me before, I thought
I had hurt or broken her. 'It's
alright,' she said, 'It's alright,'
but it never was, not for another thirty years yet, not

until you and I met, and the wheel
left me, here, in this openness, on a
morning like this one, trying like that
old crow to sing it out, let it all
go, the pain and the confusion and the
embarrassment of it, the regrets and the
damage and the stubborn, un-
trackable grieving, into this sudden light.

Looking for a Friend in the Mountains and Not Finding Her

parsley
shooting already, coriander
almost gone to seed, grass
lank and riddled with dandelion,
bean plants to the knees,
lemon in blossom,
banksia like a daylight lantern,
off to the north
the low, blue mountains
stretching for a thousand miles

No Poem for Weeks Now

No poem for weeks now, I don't know why – the
flood of things – then suddenly, tonight, just
after 1 a.m.,
from the other end of the house, you
singing under your breath, so
quietly that, through the rain, the
sound of the heater, trucks
on the highway changing gear, I can
barely hear but
do and
close my eyes, breathe
outward, slowly, a breath it
seems I have held for years.

Dust

When I came back
after almost a month away
a wild wind had damaged the roofs of neighbouring houses
and brought down the cherry laurel in our yard
and there was a fine layer of dust over everything: dust
in the cupboards, dust in the drawers, dust beneath the
     dried, cut roses,
dust in the cups and glasses, dust in shoes,
the dust of our neighbours, the dust of the city, the dust
of last year's harvest, dust of the Simpson Desert
two thousand kilometres west.

What's there to say?

Sometimes, as I talk, I feel the dust
creeping through my sentences, thoughts
turning to fine powder
as they wend through the motes of it:
theories, philosophies, histories.

Our dreams
are dust, our loves
are dust, the things
we fight for
are dust.

In the Taj Mahal
they are sweeping the dust: in the Pentagon,
the Vatican, the Louvre. In Padna

Emiliano is ploughing the dust; in Hay the sheep
are straggling through dust; in Canberra
the Prime Minister is coughing
because of the dust; outside
the wind and the birds are crying
because of their burden of dust: crying
or singing, I don't know (the world
flows through our sentences, sometimes it sings).

In the evening, the dust
turns red in the sunset: there are
worlds up there,
and centuries,
great palaces, great temples, great
archives of dust.

The past
is dust.
The future
is dust

coating
the tips of our fingers,
gathering
under the dry, cut roses

burning
as the world
turns away from us
angry beyond measure.

Hades

Nearly a decade since we've spoken
but still sometimes you come again, last
night in a dream, that after dinner I go out
to the office, though I know you know it isn't that, and when
I come back it seems it's to an empty house.

I walk through, calling your name,
but there's only
a message on a mobile phone,
soft and intimate
as if you're speaking to a lover.

At last you appear – you've
been sleeping, you say –
and explain
how wrong I am about the message.
But there's so much that isn't said.

It's cold outside,
almost winter, the kind of cold
that must have forced Persephone underground, to a
    warmth
I've only just now realised
Hades must have had.

Tinnitus

The cicadas have entered my head,
I don't know why,
growing louder through the day,
worst when sleep is bad,

their shrill silver ristling
filling every moment,
the heat and the hills they bring
mocking every comment,

ironising everything I think or do.
Always here, always also away,
it is as if I were perpetually two,
as if anything you'd say you must say

also to the trees, the heat, the metal sky.
Pulsing with the blood's pulse, holding the heart firm,
they tell me that there is no stopping them,
that they are going to be with me 'til I die.

At the University

The university
and the smell of ancient error
coming even from the trees,
the rictus in these laughing faces, young
gazelles to the slaughter.

All this unconscious machinery of death.
Five hundred thousand years
to stand an inch or two
taller, grow
fatter, live
forty years longer
but for what? To feel
the same jealousies, the same
ancient lusts?

eating our way
mindless through all
the creatures of the earth
as if we were not one of them
or the ability to talk, remember, flush our scat
brought us somehow closer to a supreme being who,
if ever it existed as anything other
than part of our perverse mathematics of
sublimation and denial
would turn, and shudder at the thought of us.

Her Feet

I take a photograph of her feet
and want to write about them, must,
so delicate they appear
in the dove-grey light, as if
a detail from a lost Vermeer
four centuries ago.

And, yes, I know
about the fetish, the not-seeing-her-whole; it's just
that when I look at them I think of all
the places they have carried her
and how they have brought her at last
here and to me.

Placed there, in the shadow under the chair,
it is as if they are listening to a distant music,
or remembering, as they make me do,
the smell of old stone or
long summer grass, at dusk, above
a house we are returning to, a home somewhere.

The Assassination of Benazir Bhutto

Taking a leaf from Salman Rushdie
the military government of Pakistan
has resorted to magic realism,
asking us to believe that the late and, at the time,
doubtless soon-to-be-elected
leader of their opposition, Benazir Bhutto,
was not assassinated at a political rally
but in fact killed herself by striking her head
sharply on the corner of her vehicle's
sun roof while ducking an imaginary bullet.
Sooner believe that blood from her
several imaginary exit wounds
left the Rawalpindi General Hospital,
entered the crowded streets,
found its way to the dusty highway and,
weaving through the feet of goats and camels, elephants
and roadside chapati vendors and
avoiding the tyres of military convoys,
made its way to Islamabad where,
climbing the steps of the presidential palace
and crossing the carpeted halls
it pooled at last at the feet of
General X, who for weeks now
has not been able to pick up a waterglass,
sign an official document,
or touch the cheek of his
beloved granddaughter
without leaving a stain.

Crows

I wake, late at night, it must be 4 a.m.,
and the words are back, demanding attention
like a murder of unwelcome crows
shaken loose by a dream, a young boy
broken into the house, the wild kid
from down the road. At last
I corner him and lock him in
the bathroom while we try to decide
what to do with him.
                              I should
call the police, I know, but know I won't, this
angry boy with the mad drunken mother
and that car-thief friend who treats him like a brother,
which he may well be, both
trying to steal what she can't give. Nothing
about a dream, they say, that isn't
in the self somehow: crows, wild boy, car-thief, mum.

Vivaldi: Concerto for Cello, Strings and Basso Continuo

Morning, with sunshine and young lovers,
in Anna's parents' holiday house
at Tambour on the far South Coast, nineteen-
seventy-one I think, her father
reading the *Canberra Times* and her mother talking
while she, big-eyed, big-jawed and pencil-thin,
sitting on Luke's lap and quietly finishing
her baked-beans-on-toast, winks
impishly at me as I enter the room, grins, while Luke,
long-blond-haired and beaming,
signals unambiguously from behind, and I
can't feel anything but companion pleasure, my
own girlfriend still sleeping
on the mattress in the shed, the day
about to spread, like the two to come, in a languid
atmosphere of ganja and the Grateful Dead – all
music it was then, all
music, all a wild
and mischievous innocence
caught on the wide, full lips of time
before the jungle of future come: a year
later and a marriage, three months
before their child Daniel was born; Anna and I
lying briefly and broken on a floor somewhere, Luke
gone for the seventh time
in his beloved panel van, foot
planted firmly to the floor, guitar

and surfboard in the back, double-
shuffling through the tight Clyde Mountain curves.

Twenty years later, it must have been, she came
to visit, matronly, a country lawyer, Daniel
now twenty-one, just
finishing his degree, my then wife-to-be
not wanting to know about such parts of me,
Luke's name on a poster on the Parramatta Road: was he
still playing James Taylor, Jackson Browne? – and is he now,
another twenty years on,
still doing so, as if
no time has ever really gone? Anna
a senior partner in a legal firm, Daniel
running for state parliament ... What
are these taut and wild confusions, this
shimmering light, these exquisite
tensions of quavers, these
tumbling and golden constellations
if they are not memory?

Winter Longing Poem

Though I leave all the doors
and windows open,
my longing for you
will not leave this house.

The Ten Towns Down

Those sounds again, each night,
over and over as the dark unfolds, great
punchings and shudderings of air, as if
squadrons of dragons were taking flight,

such screechings and clangings as might attest
the closing of the seven gates of Hell,
thunderings, like the stampede
of a thousand wildebeest

or moanings, like the lonely
calvings of a glacier – but no, it's only
the coal train from Lithgow
as it crests the range, begins the slow

descent towards Sydney, hauls
its thousand tonnes of cold black fire
through Katoomba, Leura, Wentworth Falls
and our dreams with them, all the ten towns down.

Night Rain

Night rain
washing the mountains again
reminding us all of the sea we can't have,
just like the sea does,
just like the sea.

Croesus

With delicate fingers and long silvery nails
– Arthur Rimbaud[ii]

Sometimes, late at night, as I
sit at the desk by the window, she
comes to stand behind me, rests
my shaven head against her and,
as we talk, inspects the
pores of my scalp
for the grime of the day,
squeezing them
between the nails of her
thumb and forefinger, wiping
whatever she finds
away.

We fall silent. Minutes
pass, and minutes. She
is finding things
where they don't exist. The night
deepens, stars
reappear. I am
Croesus
amongst his millions, each
small, sharp pain a
diamond, a
needle of unimagined light.

September

September

Straight
from the flight
it's as if my sight is hypersensitised, flooded
by the thick late-summer light, the figs
gravid on the boughs, grapes
almost over-ready, the lavender
alive with bees.
In the dark kitchen, a small
mountain of fresh-picked tomatoes
glows in a wicker basket, and Nona,
telling me about the season,
runs her fingers through a bowl
of just-husked beans
to show me how fat they are, each one
a living gemstone, agate
veined with purple. There's frozen spinach too,
Maria says, we have to eat
to make way for the rest, and an abundance
of pale green peppers
ready for roasting.
Eight hours later, in
bed at last, your breasts
and belly
are firm fruit in my hands,
your back, your neck, your shoulders
taste of sun.

Eagles

Gliding in
from Korte, riding
the thermals along the northern ridge
one a half-kilometre behind the other,
going home,
dwindling into the distance
in such taut synchrony;
ten minutes or more I've watched them
and scarcely a movement of their wings,
looking down
a thousand feet
into the heart of things.

Wasps

I have been getting used to them, the wasps,
here each morning over any fruit left out
telling me which peach is sweetest, which apple to cut,

chasing me from stove or reading chair,
exploring the old stone walls for cavity,
clearing great spaces for themselves in air.

Now one has bitten my cheek
and the sting's infected,
the venom's been working through me all week.

Tant pis.
It's only fitting.
I've killed a hundred in my time, at least.

Nona[iii]

Nona begins things,
a kind of midwife to the day,
up always by 5.40,
leaving her room at 6 a.m., just
as the bells start at St Blaza's,
to let the dog and the cat out, make the tea, cut
sandwiches, slice the bread and cheese.
By the time I'm up, two hours later,
she's made the *minestra*, picked salad greens, fed
hens, aired rooms, done
more than a dozen other things
and is sitting almost motionless by the
heater at the southern window, in her
daily grey,
thinking of God-knows-what, perhaps olives, perhaps
the garden, perhaps her husband, dead
these forty years, perhaps
her son, now sixty, out
in the olive groves somewhere, the winter light
on his shoulders, the wind
tugging at his thinning hair.

Like him
she likes chocolate, different cheeses, can tell
one grade of fresh-pressed
oil from another
at more than a dozen paces, though
unlike him
sleeps poorly. Her back

and her hips, she says, are slowly killing her. When
she goes
it will be with all due ceremony, another part
of the village
will flap untended in the Boria, another
house lose its hold.

Carmen 192

Your mother, in her incomprehensible denial,
has let that fingering, manipulative priest
sleep in our bed.

You're right: it's time
to drag it out into a field somewhere
and burn it.

On First Hearing of a Friend's Illness
I.M. Noel Rowe

This morning
climbing the stairs
I heard a rooster
crowing an early noon
and somebody tuning a radio somewhere,
moving from station to station,
the shrill sound
of the swallows
darting about the telephone wires,
then someone shunting bricks,
Emiliano
driving up on his tractor,
Franz
starting his old car
and turning it off again, going back inside – all this
in just a few
seconds
before nothing,
only the sound
of waiting,
if that has any sound at all.

Swallows

4 p.m., the hour
of the hundred swallows,
skimming the sky-coloured pool.

How hard
to write the simplest things,
these sabre-sharp wings
severing words from their stems.

Priest

Early in the 1990s, that pederast priest
lost part of what you might have called a heart
to a thirteen-year-old girl
now safely married and gone.

Almost twenty-one years on,
he still slurs his masses under the mountain,
tries to drown what is left of whatever it was
under a tide of schnapps

as if it were a malicious machine or
angry cat. Inconscient,
the once-thirteen-year-old's mother
still does his laundry.

An old man in
carpet slippers
sometimes tries his lock.
The tide is up to his neck.

Pumpkins on the Koper Road

Almost always there is something
flickering on the edge of our attention, like someone
at the back of a crowd, trying to catch our eye.
Sometimes it delivers its message, some-
times it doesn't.
                    This last three months or so
there has been a long row of pumpkins
in a farmer's field, running parallel to the highway
just on the edge of town, almost exactly where
the back-up from the first traffic light
draws you to a stop and holds you
for a minute or two before the next green
ushers you further down.
                    At first
it was nothing more than a set
of pale-orange glimpses amongst the large,
dark leaves against a phalanx of
ripening corn, but each time I've passed
they've been larger, for so long now
that at some point three or four weeks ago
I found myself marvelling at their size
and, since then, as we've driven by, haven't
been able to take my eyes away.
                    He must,
I thought, be growing them for the local show
or aiming for some personal best, or to out-grow
some neighbour. But no. After a few enquiries
I've learned that the farmer
is seven weeks dead, and there is just
no son or daughter to pick them.

38

Earlier this summer, walking through a different field
I came across a pumpkin of just that kind.
From the front it seemed quite normal, large and
ripe and beautiful, but when I walked around
I found a wide, black hole where some creature
had broken in and emptied it, and, bending down,
caught, I thought, the strong, sharp smell of rat.

The old man's funeral was two months ago. The corn
is yellowing now, and the great orange globes
have probably long stopped growing. Whether some creature
has hollowed them I'd have to trespass to know.
The mystical significance of pumpkins quite
escapes me. But maybe that's the point: that it's
one of the businesses of things to go, one of
the businesses of poets to try to hold them.

August

No wind, and yet
a flock of tiny
sparrows
drifting
to the road like leaves.

Ljubljana in the Sun

Like a young woman
sexually abused by her grandfather,
whose brothers care for little else but money,
whose father, the hunter, has been running
guns to neighbouring countries
and whose murderer great uncle, hiding out
for fifty years in South America,
has now sent his children home
to take over the family business,
and who, with her soft hands and
wide, almost-innocent eyes,
has just decided that she might well have –
and she may not be wrong –
the most beautiful legs in all of Europe,
Ljubljana lies basking in the sun.

The Landing

Day after golden day, thrall
to dust motes and the spars of light, a young boy
treks in the sand hills of the stars, wanders
through forests in the ancient steps,

slips through the trunks of their grain, listening
for the lumbering of beasts in the undergrowth,
the cries of natives, the macaws there, breathing
the rich, moist odours of vegetation and of earth;

and should his mother call from two flights above
into the echoing cavern of the stair,
he can look up and her face will be there,
a fellow adventurer, companion in perpetuum.

Now and again some neighbour will come
heavy with shopping from the street, or jug
of glistening water from the courtyard well
and speak to him, as if in payment to a troll,

but mostly he is alone, in the warm
dust and the tiered air, the old stone
breathing about him, and the brooding silence, such
palaces, such kingdoms there.

And if someday, decades away, an ageing, foreign-
seeming man should come, through the grace and
accident of time – myself say, looking
for an ancient apartment and a name

written on paper in a trembling hand – and,
remembering nothing, be strangely halted
by the dust and filtered light, the whisper
of the well no longer there,

and if his heart, trans-
fused, should open like a hand
into which someone is suddenly pouring grain,
what would that be? return? a poem? a life come back?

The River

Rare mornings the river is almost
palpable, high over us, the strength
of its current
pulling the clouds, the summer bells,
although most other days
it's no more than the shrunken Ljubljanica
crawling where the city channels it, algae-
thickened and sluggish
between the stone banks and the seven bridges,
creeping up walls, rotting woodwork, half-
filling glasses and coffee cups
left out while Ljubljana is sleeping.

There are
rumours of a swan
on Trubarjeva
and in the cobbled lanes off Mestni Square
though whether escaped from a butcher somewhere
or fallen into dank reason from the high, marshy
spaces above the archbishopric
isn't anything like clear.

Who, after all,
the 30th of June, 2010, would dare
to slaughter a swan (seeing her
on the clearest nights
gliding there
beyond the constellation of the Bear)?

Ah, well …

The Swan

Although
there is at least one man
who would say that, if just once and
only in a dream, he'd witnessed
something pale and creature-like
between the long and
slender thighs of a
woman from Wolfova Street, the white
swan of Ljubljana – alien and yet
night-canny, so
grimy he might almost
be a black one – is seen, if just
until that very thought arrives,
only by drowsy street-cleaners
and drunken would-be poets
waking on city benches at dawn,
foraging as at that time he does
for bits of olive or capsicum or pizza-crust
beneath the outdoor café tables
or dragging with his scarlet beak
into the first light on Polianska Street
one of the heels of bilge-
softened bread the ancient
mushroom-sellers leave for him
at the murky feet of the east-side
pylons of the Dragon Bridge.

If there
is a god, as some would say
there always is within a swan, it is, as these
might testify, were they
ever to look into his convex eye,
one of the small ones, gaunt
and terrified, starved
of its true habitat, endangered, almost
on the verge of extinction.

Olives

Dull light this afternoon
swallowing the ridges,
the sound of hunters
from the wood below Sveti Peter.
The mind wanders.
At one point I thought I heard
distant thunder
and the first drops of rain,
but it was Marco
pouring olives into the plastic bin,
the sound of Marian
starting to pick again.

Pears

It's the fourth of July in Australia
but still the third here, the night hot
and the full moon rising over Nova Vas;
she is lying back in the deckchair
trying to work out her new mobile phone
and I'm inspecting the ruins of my
backpack, caught in airport machinery
at Frankfurt or Helsinki, hardly
a problem, now I think about it,
given the mess I've just flown above,
the shelling of innocent civilians,
the bombs in the crowded markets,
asylum boats foundering in the Indian Ocean,
whales dying from explosive harpoons,
elephants falling to their knees
shot for their tusks, the cattle
and the sheep filed to their
deaths in the great Satanic
Mills of the slaughterhouses, and suddenly
Emiliano comes up, with a
basket of pears, maybe fifty
or sixty of them, all perfect, each
one the size of young child's fist,
wanting us just to see them, I guess, how
beautiful they are, with the first
russet blush of summer on them, and I
take one as he leaves, as he
wants me to, walk
over to the balcony wall

and stand there, eating it, stare
out at the distant lights of the villages,
making no sense of anything,
engulfed in mystery.

A Month of Seven Funerals

I'm sitting in the study long after dinner, still
thinking, and at some point Bobbi
on his mat beside the desk
lets out a strange howl in his dog dream
and I wonder if it could possibly be
that he knows that this has been
a month of seven funerals,
and then smile, imagining him looking up
and, seeing my long face,
wondering if it could possibly be
that *I* sense, somehow, what *he* is feeling.

The night gets deeper, anyway, and at a later point
I take him down the inside stairs
so that he can sleep the rest of it
in his favourite place under the kitchen table
then come back up myself, thinking
of going to bed, and of my small
and scattered handful of friends
and of all the sad things that scatter us.

Late Music

Late music
from a party in the village
and the voices of children returning home
speaking about the new priest, drunk
in his own vomit
at the bottom of the rectory stair, the yellow moon
leering over Grintovec, bats
swooping the streetlight,
a boar in the valley
braying loudly for a mate.

Apricots

Some years it's the tomatoes
red and thick on the trellises,
some years it's the small, sweet grapes
hanging over the outside table,
some years the golden potatoes
thick in the sandy field,
some years, dry years, it's apricots,
small and intense
weighing down the boughs,
drawing the wasps in,
filling the air with their yellowness,
and always, always it's olives
dozing through the hot summer,
waking when the autumn tightens,
tumbling from the nets into the open bins:
I sometimes think
it's the heart that the crops respond to
as much as the drift of seasons,
one year's memories bringing on
the next year's attentions,
the year after's harvest; a memory, say, of his mother's
golden chips on a winter Sunday, or the way
his father, just after the war
would reach up from the table
to pull the black grapes down, and he
and his brothers, and the wives and the cousins talked,
or the way,
on one of his summer leaves from the army,
that strange, slender girl, Alenka, dead

now these forty-two years,
gathered a dozen apricots
then sat there, with the pile of them
golden in her lap,
breaking them in halves
and giving them to him, the halves,
one by one, between her lips,
gripped by the tips of her teeth.

Witness

You're spared, for
something, as
witness. Not
knowing what
will be of help. No
thought to
who might hear. That
vineyard there – the long
rectangle of
striated green – planted
with money from the
dictator; that
story you heard
yesterday
about the young
poet in Buchenwald
who could do nothing after
but drink and
wander; this bright
morning with its melon and
peaches
warm from the sun; the
panic
in the young cow's eye; you
cannot not
utter you must
say, and say.

Open House

In the Kingdom of Shadows

In the back lanes and alleyways
a few late humans are scuttling off
abandoned by their bicycles
but don't worry, they

are diurnal, if we
don't frighten them
they will flow eventually over us
like slow, tainted light.

In the kingdom of shadows,
in the march of the middle night,
the last embers of the day gone out,
the puppets are lost in their stupors of desire.

In the kingdom of shadows, world without end,
slugs traverse the prairies of the soul,
mice enter the pure land,
cockroaches conquer the valleys of death.

In the kingdom of shadows, dominion
of cats and sugar gliders,
moths are mastering the constellations, spiders
whispering their histories to the stars.

Spiders About the House

Up here it's funnel-web country,
build a house and it draws them around,
every basement a Chartres or a Coventry,
every low window a trawling-ground:
garden with gloves on, take care
when you're under the deck,
touch a trip-wire and you summon them,
move a log too quickly
and one might leap at your neck.
They come up through the floorboards
to escape the wet, roam widely in springtime
looking for a mate, can get aggressive
when whatever passes for their blood is up.
I don't like to kill anyone, deadly or not,
but I draw a line at my thresholds:
any such neighbour that crosses them
might be neighbour no more.
Perhaps the best that you can say
is that funnel-webs keep red-backs away,
though very few others: certainly not the wolf spiders
who riddle our lawn with their burrows
and can be seen out hunting at night,
their emerald eyes glinting in torchlight,
or the St Andrew's Cross, with their great wide
web outside the back door, my
almost favourite, so
perfect the X they make of themselves, right
at the centre, like men spread-
eagled in the middle of their being

or ski jumpers at the top of their flight, second only
to the mystic orb-spider whose intricate tracery
between the wormwood and the lemon tree
is such a metaphor for poetry.
And yet there are more – the daddy-long-legs, say,
supposedly most poisonous of all
were he ever able to get fangs through skin
or the tiny, tentative swimmer I found in
the bathroom sink last winter, who stayed
three days or so, savouring the splash
of surf, the waves, thirsty beyond measure
for something I suspect there is no measuring,
or those other two, internal and, I guess, my
point in writing this: the one
whose web you see only on the MRI, the neat
bundles of her victims at C2 or 3 (you
never see the spider herself, but feel her, late at night,
testing the guy-ropes, patrolling
the trip-wires, tugging here and there where
something on a nerve needs tightening), and
this last one, stranger still,
whose web's his life itself: damaged
and torn, repaired a hundred times, ob-
ssessive beyond imagining, he'll
lumber out at almost any trouble or
excitement in his neighbourhood,
wrap it clumsily in a
cocoon of words, as if he thought it could
be kept, or understood.

Eight Mile

In the house on the ridge
at the Eight Mile, on the old veranda,
people are talking
late into the night,
about suffering and memory, history, loss,
the comings and the goings of love,
the rights of the living and the dead.
A three-quarter moon
rises and lingers overhead
and is slowly covered by cloud;
wind picks up and then calms.
Unnoticed, a young possum
sits a long while in a tree-fork, watching.

Someone stands, goes inside,
comes back with another bottle.

The sky clears.
The moon
shines down again.
Somewhere in the trees below
a night bird swoops, catches something,
takes it away.

Tips of cigarettes
glow in the dark.

The talk continues.

A Call from Mandelstam

… Osip
Mandelstam that is, great
Russian poet, died
in exile in Siberia, 1938: I'm
standing in the kitchen, 1 a.m., doing
the last of the washing-up, staring
out through the window
at first at the night's great blackness, then
at the delicately scalloped underwing
of a snow-white moth
almost as big as the palm of my hand
crawling slowly over the upper pane, the
intricate articulation of the legs, the
albino redness of the eyes, when I get
this sudden urge for *poetry*,
so strong it's like an addict's doubling.
I don't drop everything, of course, since
everything is nearly done,
but rinse the last pot and put it on the rack, drain
the water, dry my hands, then
glancing back at the window as if
the moth might just have a clue for me
go in to the bookcase in the living room
where we've put almost all of the poetry,
but whatever it is that is calling me
certainly isn't there. It isn't
Yeats, it isn't Pound, it isn't John Clare,
isn't Lorca, isn't Miłosz, isn't Strand,
isn't James Baxter, isn't Merwin, isn't Bly, shelf

after shelf, nearly a thousand books, and nothing
seems to be reaching me, nothing responds. I
turn to the Australians but it's the same thing again,
not Wright, not Hope, not Adamson, not J.S. Harry – even
my beloved Chinese are not helping me tonight,
not Tu Fu, not Wang Wei, not Li Po, not Po Chű-I,
though in frustration I'm about to take my ancient
Penguin Book of Chinese Verse when I remember, without
much hope or enthusiasm, the musty set
of *Modern European Poets*
at ground-level under the ornaments on the
far side of the room, but it's not Pavese, not Cendrars,
not Blok, not Yevtushenko, not Celan, so much
horror, so much sadness there, yet the wanting
is almost an aching in my belly now;
then, just as I'm about to stand, my eye
catches the spine of Osip Mandelstam and something
draws my hand, almost despite itself. I reflect
a little guiltily that I remember almost nothing about him, have
never even opened the book, yellow
and dog-eared as this copy is, so
I take it – what else to do? – and go upstairs, sit
on the edge of the bed, pull
off my shoes and
socks and
open it at random,
and there it is, page 64, poem one hundred and
twenty-seven: *'For life'*, it says, *'for life
and care,
I'll give up everything.
A kitchen match could keep me warm.'*

Indian Mynahs

For years now the Indian Mynahs, garbage-
bag-peckers, mowers
of young parsley or basil plants, constructors
of 'untidy clusters of dried grass and twigs
in the crevices of buildings',
have been taking over the suburb, chasing
the sparrows and pigeons out, repelling
the bulbuls, driving
even the currawongs away.
Frequently since mid December
I've seen a pair of them
fossick about in the garden, go off
with grass fronds, twigs from the ash tree,
bits of dried dandelion with the heads still intact, scraps
of string or paper, whisps of hair
to build up a nest somewhere
then heard them, in the early morning,
as I'm making the coffee, perch
high up behind the stove
on the ledge of the exhaust fan vent
to look out for a while
at the sun rising over Annandale
as unperturbed by the noise within
as I am by theirs.

They work so cannily. Five
days away over Christmas – wild
winds, high temperatures, fires
all down the eastern seaboard –

and we come back
through the long gauntlets of flame
to an exhaust fan that doesn't work, choked
to a standstill by a large, flat nest
made of all the things we've watched them gathering
and at the side of it, perched
neatly atop a sealed-off exit-pipe
as if it were a custom-made eggcup, one pale
blue egg, the colour of Chinese porcelain – a poem
given, clearly enough, but also
an object-lesson in the art itself,
how you need a ledge or alcove
to lodge a poem in, how you
build it with whatever comes to hand,
stalks of dried dandelion, say, or bird feathers, twigs
of memory, fragments
of half-forgotten, sky-blue pleasure, and try to weave them
    together
as some birds do
into a round, well-crafted thing
though as often as not find you have simply
piled them
one on the other
like the Indian Mynahs,
leaving the eggs to the reader.

Looking for Andrei Gromyko

Standing in the shower this morning,
getting ready to go in to work
I thought suddenly of Andrei Gromyko.
I can't say why. All I'd been doing
was answering an email about a new
professor of Australian Literature and preparing
to send a friend's translation of Catullus to a publisher
and while I might have been briefly thinking
of Memmius and Gellius and the rise
and fall of Caesars, poets
fiddling while Rome burns, etc.,
I was also making a second pot
of coffee and wiping up birdshit from the
kitchen floor and I can't quite see what Andrei Gromyko
had to do with any of that: this is
Australia after all and there have never been
any Andrei Gromykos here. Maybe
it was a dream I'd had, maybe
it is something in the air, but all
day it's obsessed me. I asked my wife if she could explain it
and she said 'Andrei who?' I asked my class, all
twenty-four students, but none of them
knew who Gromyko was either.
He was not in the Mitchell Library
where I went to meet a friend at lunchtime.
He was not in the Australian Museum,
nor, as far as I could tell, in any
of the coffee shops along Broadway or Glebe Point Road
and if eventually I thought I saw him

in a meeting of the Professorial Board
he blurred so quickly it was impossible to tell.

I looked in the papers
but there was nothing there. I listened to the news
and some inane talk-back radio, but while
I did learn something about baking and people's opinions
on recycling water from sewage treatment plants
there was no sign of Gromyko anywhere, nor later
when I walked the dog or went to the wine shop or
talked to Tom Petsaninis for half an hour in the
middle of Darghan Street, or from my study window
watched a drug deal going down in the
alley behind the house. The absence of Gromyko
is becoming overwhelming: I seem
to be not seeing him everywhere.
Even the potato-like visage
of the Australian Prime Minister on the evening news
and the narrow, myopic eyes of the National Treasurer
can't quite explain it, though by this time
I've thought of Gromyko so often that his bald head
and zip-tight lips might almost be said
to be drifting before me in the twilight.

Later, in bed, the name
is still ringing so much within me
that, just to get rid of it, I imagine
climbing out through the window
and shouting it from the bathroom roof,
and all the small creatures of the night
scuttling off into their dark reaches,
the moths and the spiders and the cockroaches,

going *Andrei Gromyko!*   *Andrei Gromyko!*   *Andrei Gromyko!*
as if carrying to all their towns and villages
tidings of some new, distant star.

But I don't, of course,
and it isn't like that.

Sometimes
I hear screaming.
Sometimes I hear wild shouting.
Sometimes, late at night, I hear
knocking
from the house next door,
knocking
and knocking …

Phasmid

They call them *Phasmatidae*, I think, the genus,
though I might well be wrong;
the *species* I simply cannot trace: small
stick-like insects so perfectly disguised
you'd think them a part of a eucalypt until,
the wind or some sudden
disturbance of the leaves dislodging them, they fall
onto something not their colour. Match-length
scrolls of bark, they could be, though looking more closely
you think something more delicate, utterly.

I'd see one once or twice a year
fallen from the great gum tree
at the bottom of the Creek Street yard,
little vessels of dust, moving through the same,
but never, before or since, any one like this, pre-
ternatural, primordial, a Titan amongst insects, dinosaur, some
twenty-two centimetres long
on the concrete floor of the garage; at first I thought
a stick, but, going to kick it aside
saw her move, just slightly, and realised.

When I came back, driving carefully,
she was no longer there,
though two days later I saw her again
clinging to the rubber tyre
of a car parked in the lane:
there must have been a mighty
power in her legs, to hold her there, so horizontally,

and of course I feared for her, and should have left
a note for the driver before taking off,
but didn't, being in some human rush.

The next day the car was gone
and the creature also from my mind until,
driving in again, a few days later still,
and getting out of the car, I saw her
lying less than a metre from me, her hind-part
just crushed by my driver's-side wheel.
I picked her up, of course, and buried her beneath
the tree from which I've always thought she came
and since then, for eleven years or more, I've
wondered what could be their name.

Ninox strenua

Ninox strenua, the Powerful Owls, stand
sixty centimetres tall and have wingspans
of almost one hundred and fifty, 'defend'
a territory of up to fifteen hundred hectares
though hunt much wider. Have beaks
tough as boltcutters, mate for life, live
on a diet of ringtailed possum and sweet
sugar glider, are endangered and rarely seen
though their two-note call is familiar
to anyone who listens to the bush at night.
In our catchment there's at least one breeding pair,
working its way as the months pass
anti-clockwise over an area twenty by
twenty kilometres – four hundred square.
The local wildlife rescue service
will not release young possums into the scrub
at any time near the full moon and until
they've checked the raptor's whereabouts.
Ninox strenua are rumoured to kill
up to thirty ringtailed possums each per night, and, almost
human in their wastefulness,
eat only the brain.

Open House

Birds, she murmurs, and goes on writing,
then, later, *birds* again
before standing up
and going off to bed
as if something has at last been said.

In the sudden silence afterward
there are no birds to be heard,
only the deep thrumming of the body
like some huge vessel
moving slowly towards open water

the doors
and windows of the house
so open now
almost anything might enter

The Barbarians

I have known these families
upwards of a year now, new
neighbours in a rented house, generation
after generation, children and parents, grand-
parents and beyond. Coming in
each night from under the skirtings
to graze on the dry dogfood, striking out
over the white tiles of the kitchen floor
looking always for something more,
they can seem a kind of sluggish centaur
or young, just-antlered elk
crossing fresh-fallen snow
leaving their silver trails
so thickly on the entrance mat
you'd think it a magic carpet or
homage to the Milky Way.

In an earlier house, not long ago,
fearing for my precious lettuces
I'd have sprinkled salt on them
or caught them up in a paper towel
and left them outside for the birds,
but now, in what must be
a joke as much for them as me, I
coax them onto leftover salad leaves
and take them carefully into the long grass

at the bottom of our tiny yard, hoping
that the birds won't find them, well aware
they'll make their way back
the next night, or the night after that.

Tonight there are at least eleven of them
gathered about his bowl, chowing down
ravenously, as if they've come
from a long hike somewhere – a wedding, say,
in the house next door, or funeral
on the far side of the patio.

Looking down, from my human height,
they seem a world away; 'we are not
compatible', I'm tempted to say; 'wherever they go
is not where I would go';
'we are as different as moon and sun',

then, shocked, stop myself, seeing
at last how the barbarians come.

Freight

A hot night,
no sign of the promised storm.
You argue with your parents
long distance – that
bloody priest again – and then
go out to the deck
to watch the quarter moon
ride the clouds westward.
So much
still left unsaid – the bed
so full of ghosts
we hold each other
waiting for sleep to blanket them.

At 3 a.m. – your breathing
calm and deeper now – something
triggers the porch light
and I hear the scream
of some small creature
cut suddenly off: just
that, no
wing-sound, no
scuttering of cat

and then, five
minutes later, the long
slow ache of a freight train,
and the starting rain.

Cold Mountain

at it again
air thick with rain and midnight
shoes soaked from the wet grass

flap, flap of its wings
as it shifts to the cherry laurel
to watch the point of my torchlight

The Plover

There's a fellow crying in Martin Place. They can't stop him.
— LES A. MURRAY[iv]

There's a Spur-winged Plover
holding up traffic on Ross Street
right in the middle of the southbound lane.
Cars and buses, vans and taxis, pick-ups and four-wheel drives
all the way back to the Anzac Bridge
and more of them coming.
There's a Spur-winged Plover
holding up traffic on Ross Street,
right in front of an old red Volvo,
no-one can budge her.

Drivers are getting out of their vehicles,
passengers are angling for a better view,
diners are sidling out of Tran's Thainese
with spring rolls and napkins in their hands,
tattooists and half-finished customers
wandering out of Needles-R-Us.
What's the hold-up? An accident? A pedestrian down?
Someone dying in the street? But no,
it's only a bird, a Spur-winged Plover, screaming incessantly,
refusing to let anyone near her.

'Run over the bastard!' calls a large man in a business suit,
but then shrinks back into the crowd
shamed by the glare of his neighbours;
'Cut off its head', cries a young girl, mimicking,

then ducks, as if an invisible hand had swiped at her,
or the bird were protected by ring of fire.
No thought, no daring, no tenderness
can enter the plover's wide circle of fury;
any attempt is answered by a wild rush
and a wide-beaked, demonic cry.

'I've had enough!' she seems to be shrieking,
'and I'm not going to take it anymore!
I'm sick of the traffic!
I'm sick of the buildings!
I'm sick of this city!   y
I'm sick of people!   a
I'm sick of pollution!   w
I'm sick of everything!'   a
– but these are only imaginings: no-one could guess
the true secret of the bird's distress.

                                                        and

Later, people will say she was disoriented, lost,
or that she was merely defending her nest,   flaps
but they will not have seen the frenzy in her eye.
Still others will claim they gathered her,   ty
calmed her, took her to the Bay, but it isn't that way.   twen
As if, quite suddenly, there was no more to say
and no point in shouting at humans anyway,   teen
the bird simply stops, composes herself, makes   eigh
one last rush at the dumbfounded Volvo, then,   teen
avoiding the hands reaching up for her, takes off,   six

Jennifer's Mound

It was that time again: almost out of meat and
seven pigs fattening at an alarming rate. A house meeting
and it was decided, Jennifer it would have to be, the
oldest and largest, or Two-spot, the next in size, though it
    had been
such a hassle to get the last one down the mountain for the
    killing
we decided we would try to do it here – or
get it done, if Steve would come up from Radiance, a gentle
giant of a guy when he wasn't overdoing acid, a
butcher's son, and excellent with a gun
since that's the way I wanted it, quick and
painless; as the cook I guess it was my say.
And that's how it was, standing a little back
from the middle of the kitchen door, out of sight's way,
taking aim at Jenny at the centre of the yard
on the mound of dirt and gravel someone
had brought there for something they'd
never got around to, well before I came,
now all grown over with couch grass and
dandelion and dock, which for some reason
the pigs had decided they'd rather
doze upon than crop.
                       One
rifle shot and a
second of shock and she was down, as
clean as you could have wished it, dead
before she hit the ground. I should
have moved the others out

if I'd have thought of it, but didn't. We
loaded her onto a cart – much squealing then – and
took her round the front, where Steve strung her up
on the post-frame over the gate he reckoned
must have been used for that purpose before,
bled her, and slit her open, gathered her guts
in an old washing tub, cleaned her and cut her up, the rest
of them eerily silent now, huddled against the far fence
on the other side of the house.

It's not that but the next morning I'm writing about:
getting up at 5 a.m. to make coffee in the strange
quiet and the mist and, looking out,
seeing them there, all six, lying
on the mound like ghostly sentinels, their grief
as pervasive as the mist itself. They kept it up for days
and afterward migrated to the far side of the shed.

We ate her, as you have to do, out of respect, and then – it
was only weeks – I said, knowing
it was probably the end of me there, I said
That's it. I'm never cooking meat again.

Carmen 193

All day the poet writes
about the wondrous creatures of the world,
the beasts, the fishes and the birds,
their gracefulness, their speed, their flight,
then, wonder typed and safely filed,
wonders which to eat tonight.

The Roo Field

It's hard to say how they'd stacked up up there,
the barbed wire fence only chest-high, and I'm not tall:
surely nothing an average grey couldn't clear
given room to gather pace,
but I'm not a kangaroo. Probably one or two
had come first and judged against it;
there was a road after all,
and a car or truck every minute or so,
and maybe at that time just grass enough, drought
as it was, but more had come, and more,
tired and hungry, from the hills behind Tharwa,
more, and more;
by the time it became clear
that they had no option but to jump
there would have been no room for it
and all they could do was stare,
all thousand of them, a thousand plus,
at the great field of summer grass just opposite,
and I could only watch them standing there,
without food or water or space to move, packed
like sardines, I might once have said,
or humans in a soon-to-be-burning nightclub.

They were so *still*.
If I'd had a gun
I could have tried to startle them
but what good would that have done?
Even as I'd stood there more had come.
Maybe, that night, with the traffic gone

the great mob of them somehow dispersed.
I've always hoped so. And maybe
it was all and only a dream
like the one I woke from this morning,
the men and the women and the children
at the barbed wire fence, so
gaunt, in their striped uniforms.

'We pass a town empty of people'

A landscape that was all saltbush
and red sand before
is now billabongs and oxbows, riverains.
We pass a town empty of people
through a storm of fattening galahs, move out
past locusts gorged on green stubble,
a wedge-tailed eagle
feasting on road-kill kangaroo,
the desert lush as legend, wild duck
circling in their thousands over lakes
not seen since early last century, kites,
hawks and Nankeen kestrels
keeling in the heavy air,
sluggish with plenitude.

Captain Hunter and the Petrels

Tuesday the 12th of February and I've gone to see Andrew, picked
up a few things from the bookshop on the way – two
novels since I'm in that mood, a book
of paintings of Australian birds and a CD of Gurrumul
   Yunupingu
whose voice haunted me so much a year ago – then
gone to the dentist, the second time in two days,
and come home numb-jawed to read the news of how
an elderly Catholic priest with dementia has been fined
for biting the ear off another
in a fight over a parking spot. In
the bird book there's a story of how, in 1790, shipwrecked
John Hunter, the crew of the *Sirius* and Norfolk Island's five
hundred inhabitants (mostly prisoners) avoided starvation
   by eating
one hundred and seventy thousand of its nesting petrels. A
rescue ship arrived in August, but the petrel – named
'Providence' accordingly (from *providore*) –
has never recovered; the only image we have of it
was drawn by Captain Hunter himself
as his victim was on her way to the cooking pot. The book
has also several illustrations of the Mountain Lowry
and as I read about the petrels I was thinking
of the bird that hit the study window yesterday – how
we heard the *thunk* from the kitchen
just as the rain began, and went in
to find the smudge-mark on the pane and the oh-
so-beautiful lowry lying on the grass below – a

'heart break', as Teja might have said – so
still I could not imagine that he wasn't dead, but she
saw movement and ran down
and came back holding him closely to her chest
and within two minutes he had woken and
suddenly flown, leaving only, on the lawn, a single
green-blue feather, such as John Hunter might have drawn.
A poem is a place where you can bring things together, you
don't have to know why. The mad and the bad, the
gentle and the dead, tooth-ache and heart-ache
and the ache and quandary of history. We are all
creatures trembling under the sun of witness (or
is it rain?); some of us, for reasons it would be hard to explain,
trying to catch the strange, sad music of it,
on the days we can hear it,
before it disappears again.

Majesty

Resplendent
in dust and late sunlight
an old sow, tall and walking-
stick-slender from the rear, moustachioed, great
moon-fish shaped from the side, her
long, sparse hairs
and leathern hide gold-
brown in the Jaipur dusk, her
withered dugs
almost touching the ground,
has come up from the river flats
to trawl the earthen gutters for scraps
from the street-stalls – broken
melons, coconuts, pieces of naan, slops
of chana or saag paneer – while the traffic
of trucks and camels, rickshaws and rattling taxis
thins and the last, soft coronas of light
settle radiant upon
her oblivious and
many-nippled godliness:

Goddess
Sow, God
Melon, Goddess
Coconut, God
Light, Goddess
Dusk, Goddess

Street, Goddess
Dug, Goddess
Camel, God
Naan

And there, as
always, outside
Pandit's Bicycle Rent and Repair Shop, drinking
warm, strong, Mandhar's
Evaporated Milky tea, God
Order-of-things, yarning endlessly
with God Nothing-to-be-done

How to Ride a Horse

Once the hair was removed, the tanners would bate the
material by pounding dung into the skin, or soaking the
skin in a solution of animal brains.
      – Wikipedia, entry on 'Tanning'

To ride a live horse, it must be said,
you must first have a dead one,
which you have had *flayed*
to remove the *skin* or *hide*, and which then –
with the aid of an essence of oak-tree or
a sequence, less expensively,
of urine, faeces and animals brains –
you've had *cured* or *tanned*
before, dried and beaten to soften it,
you've had it cut into various lengths and shapes
for the saddle, the reins, the straps,
and the hat, belt and boots
that a rider wears (their wallet, their whip, their
watchband, their crop), the rest
of the carcase having long been consigned
to the makers of dog-food and glue.

As for the second, the living horse,
it must be *broken*, unless of course
it has been *bred in captivity*, when it may be deemed
to have been broken from the start. Saddled,
with the bit and the reins in place,
it can then be mounted and (the dead
horse on the living's back) gently

goaded by the rider's ankles, its mouth
pulled firmly to the left or right,
made to follow any track a rider might.
Stroked, occasionally, and brushed,
stalled, watered, given hay – *loved*,
as riders are wont to say – until such time
as it becomes a dead horse (etc.),
it should be of service indefinitely. (You may,
in the above, care, where
appropriate, to substitute
'dead cow' for 'dead horse'.)

Now to talk about fences …

At the Lytton Hotel,

barely
able to hear myself think
for the day-long shouting and jackhammers of the
sewer-work outside the window
and the sound of the five
trapped pups
in the service yard opposite
yelping and whining all night
and their mother incessantly
barking, the
valets in their workroom down the corridor
with their Bollywood blaring from six a.m.
and the beggars and taxi spruikers the
constant honking of the cars   telling
that man inside me *Be*
calm be
calm
and the
sound of the
five trapped pups
yelping and whining, the
poor bitch coming back
at two and three and four a.m. un-
able to get to them
with her dark swollen nipples in the
pool of
dusty light under the
streetlamp hanging so
low and heavy beneath her, so

low and
full, so
aching, so
broken, I

Plenitude

for Johanna Featherstone

It is the 4th of April, 2008, and I am thinking of pigeons
partly because Johanna has asked me, and partly because
I have just seen three
topknot pigeons
on separate telephone wires
at a cross-street by the
highway in Lawson, NSW,
and thought, of course, of Ezra Pound
seeing the swallows
on the wires of the DTC[v]
and (he not I) thinking of Janequin[vi] – how
limited that stave must have been, with half the half-
notes limitless sky (what
sound does a
swallow
make in flight, what
F, what
A?) although
all I can
think of for
now is how I
ate a pigeon once, at Gay Bilson's O-
so-expensive
restaurant at Berowra, the
cool and
grey-pink
tenderness of the
breast of it, so almost uncooked – so

rare – that I very nearly complained
and would certainly not have finished it
were it not for *the price I was paying*, and my own reputation
(though with no-one but myself) for eating almost everything –
    snake,
alligator, snail, goat, Li-river catfish, sea-squirt, roo –
as if, as I thought then, that
were something to be proud of
and not yet another of my
Seventy-Seven Stupidities.

Why
pigeons? I wonder,
and then Why
not? if the tiny
and not the immense shall
lead us (that is Webb[vii])
out of the wilderness of our human thought, then
there can be no
stopping-point (follow
a cockroach, say
into the
labyrinth of desire …)

The great
ornithologist, John James Audubon[viii],
recorded having seen, in the
autumn of 1813,
a *pass*age of migrating
Passenger Pigeons
lasting three days, so many sometimes they
filled the sky and almost

blotted out the sun. In a similar
index of plenitude, W.
G. Sebald, in the third
chapter of *The Rings of Saturn*
reproduces a photograph
of men standing up to their knees
in a tide of fresh-caught herring (I
remember that, in my
small way – the mullet-run in
Huskisson …).[ix]

Passenger, from *passager*, to
pass (they
carried nothing): rose-
pink (the male), grey-
crested, long tapered tail …

glass-
eyed, faded by
sun from the
window,
layered with
dust in the de-
commissioned display, Case
Western Reserve University,
1968

the last
Passenger Pigeon, named Martha,
died 'alone' at the
Cincinnati Zoo at around
1 p.m. on September 1st, 1914, and the

herring industry is gone.
I think of them because just
lately the Commonwealth
Government of Australia
condoned the killing
of four hundred kangaroos
in the heart of the National Capital – not
many, as far as
roo slaughter goes
but I take it as sign[x] – and now
there is talk of a 'cull'
of koalas on Kangaroo Island, another
of corellas in Gippsland, possums
in north-western Victoria, and just today (4th April, as I say) I
read that the last
Tasmanian Devil in the wild will
very likely die before
face-cancer-free replacements are ready
to be released from the laboratory

the last
Tasmanian Tiger 'in captivity' died
at the Hobart Zoo
on September 7th, 1936; the last
Tasmanian Aboriginal … ah,
but we are not to
draw such comparisons …

I try
to work out the essential
difference between
humanity and the flesh-

eating Ebola virus but can't
come up with much, the huge
ulcers of our cities
creeping over the earth, the vast
plantations to serve *our* needs
devouring everything in their path, but to
return to pigeons, though fearing
that any attention drawn to them is like
directing the sight of a gun,
I'd like to salute
Bohumil Hrabal, author of
Closely Watched Trains[xi],
who is said to have
died while
trying to feed pigeons
through a fifth-floor window
of a Czechoslovakian psychiatric hospital:

privately,
I think it was a
bold and
arguably suc-
cessful
attempt at
flight

The Gate

What are they after, those huge dogs
we see sometimes at the street gate
or through one of the boundary fences, emerging
from the dusk, the scrub, suddenly *there*,
then gone before you can call anyone
or tell for certain what breed they are, Bull-
mastiff, you'd think, though crossed
with Doberman or Arab or Great Dane? Someone's
pig-hunting dogs maybe, let loose
or just got free, roaming with impunity,
and we worry for the sheep, the ducks, the rabbits, our own
farm dog or any other creature sheltering here, waking at night
to listen for anything unusual, hair raised
at any sound of a squall, checking each morning
to make sure all are there. You see them
once or twice in a week sometimes, then maybe
just once in a month or so, but it can be much longer, and
     you forget
about telling the Council, raising the fences, asking the vet
for what she might know of them, then look up
and suddenly they are there again, tight
browed, thick jowled, black eyed, the dark
forest behind them, staring from the gate.

Wild Ducks

A splash-
landing in the pond, another then
another, another, the ducks
back after three days who knows where – flight-
training most likely, the two
ducklings just ten days ago
working like the Wright brothers on a stretch
of open ground by the water-tank: such
strange disquiet we had when they first flew off
having watched them almost from the nest,
three of them at first, struggling through the lawn, one gone
    within a day
from the cold, I imagine, of too-early spring, the others
slowly growing, thickening, there from earliest morning
pecking through the wet grass, day in and out, learning
at last to swim, the parents
always shepherding, the drake elegant, aloof, alert, the
    mother
aggressively protective, running at you open-beaked
if you came too close, one day so surprising me
that I tripped, crashed to the path,
bore the bruises and pulled muscle for a month. I
don't know where they nest – thought
the old chook-pen at first, then beneath the cabin deck, the
thick rhododendron by the pond, but no, though
we heard one night a caterwauling from somewhere there; I
    guess
she dealt with that intruder too. I
don't know why I write this, it's

all human and I can't
get out of this place, into the purportedly true, yet here we are
a sort of protectors to them, nothing more
and not well even that, marvelling at
the way they stretch their slim necks
forward with each stride
as if there were something
just there, beyond, to be knocked upon.

Report from Blue Mountains

Another Page from the Book of Everything

with the error so entrenched that we'll never root it out
with all the human evils and the good that tracks them
    like gulls following a ship at sea
with all the seas and the swelling oceans, the creeks and
    the pools and the rivers that run down to them
the Seine and the Parramatta, the Arno, the Mara
    with its swift dark current and its wooden mills,
    the Sava with its freight of bodies just shot or
    throats cut at the waterside
with the company of poets whispering their secret graft
    like old men showing each other
    their gemstones on the Ponte Vecchio
with the Ponte Vecchio, the Pont Neuf, the Rialto, the
        Harbour Bridge
    and the sludge that gropes under them,
    taking Florence and Paris and Sydney to their separate
        inseparate seas
with the intolerable and hideous weight of them
    and their paradoxical lightness, the girders and the steeples
with their infinite mysteries,
    their intricate filigrees of rust
with the human Gargantuas eating their way
    through all of the flocks of the earth,
    each day in each person
    seventeen kinds of death
with the beasts themselves caged or in pasture or transport
        trucks,
with their soft muzzles, their large innocent eyes,
    the pale whisps of their breath in the dawn fields

or by gas station lights at midnight
with the vast manscapes and the roads that lead to them
    severing and dividing the indivisible (O fields of
        illusion!)
with the wombat-holes by the highway at Lake George
    and the pomegranates overhanging the old road to
        Tressan,
    we humans stumbling about
    so dangerous in our guilt and loneliness
with the cockatoos circling and the water
    flowing into the dam, my neighbour Franklin coming out
    with his big tin of birdseed,
    pouring it into the white plastic bowl, another
lightness with its myriad strange messages, another
day with its hands wide open
another page from the book of everything

Beauty and the Beast

It's Beauty and the Beast with us, no
question, she
the Beauty and the other
there in the mirror each morning
inching towards me relentlessly, a
pock-marked, rough-skinned, frowning thing
ruddy with alcohol and thinking
asking and giving no quarter, staring at me
with eyes that know far too much
and to which there is never an answer. Why
she has stayed with me so faithfully
there is no knowing – some
aberration of her own perhaps
or predilection for ancient wood or stone: birds
choose their homes, why not she? Starling
in an ancient belfry, snowy
barn owl in a hole
high in a lightning-struck tree, the home
she makes in me
warms me indescribably, a secret
treasure I'll not relinquish
while ever the living's in me, use
every ounce of beastness to protect.

Mist

I.M. Pat Skinner

It was a Sunday afternoon
and we had taken the dog for a walk
in the park by the swimming pool –
the large park with the small brown lake trimmed with old
    pines
and bordered by the rainforest gully
with the sound of the creek running through it –
and had gone over to the open space
and thrown the ball for him
and talked to the lady with the three kelpies
and she had told us about the copperhead they had seen
    through the summer
and shown us where he lived
under the thick scrub willow
and we had made our way to the other side of the lake
and I had looked back towards her, and seen that mist had
    already covered the ridge,
and for a few moments, having wondered where the ducks
    were
and listened to the wild screeching of the cockatoos
high over the forest of stringybarks,
I turned to watch the dog
exploring the bushes by the swimming-pool fence
and when I turned back – it was
no more than ninety seconds – the mist had rolled in
and most of the lake
and all of the opposite bank had disappeared,
the opposite bank, and the trees, and the woman with her dogs,

as if a cloud had descended
as I suppose it had,
and as I was watching this – the brown, glassy lake
disappearing under the mist, and the mist thickening –
and noting the sudden quiet,
no sound of water, no dog-bark, no sound of cockatoos,
the ducks came back, two of them,
landing on the lake, with long, rippling *V*s
trailing behind them where just a moment before had been
    nothing,
and floating towards me, then curving gently away,
just that: no
solution to anything,
no end to the war, no end to stupidity,
no answer to death and dying,
no consolation

the ducks came back, that's all,
and floated across the lake,
and turned gently away

no message for me
or anyone I knew.

If Anyone Asks for Me

My home is in the mountains now,
I am becoming reclusive after all this time,

living with my young wife the painter,
enjoying cooking, drinking wine,

letting it settle the dust of too much busyness,
keeping the barking of the world at bay.

If anyone asks for me, let someone say
'He is lost among clouds'.

The Man in the Lift

As if he were a dog
reading the wind, and although
you are wearing no perfume, only the
oh-so-subtle scent of yourself, the elderly
man in the lift, just before the door
closes behind you (perhaps it does not seem
to him that we are together, you
leaving at the third-floor lobby, I
going on up to the seventh), lifts his head
slightly, closes his eyes, dilates
his nostrils
in a long, slow breath.

Broad Bean Meditation

This afternoon, at the kitchen counter, 'liberating'
just-cooked broad beans from their skins,
I found myself thinking
of the children that I never had,
and beyond them, through the mind's
deep shadows, all
the generations of the lost – aborted, mis-
carried, dead in the egg or womb
or during the hard passage out of them.
It's their shape, I guess, pale
Forms in the fingers, foetal, homuncular,
each broad bean in its caul:
one might be holding a dead star.

Pythagoras, the ancient Greek philosopher,
would not let his followers consume them,
maybe because, as Pliny said, the souls
of the dead still dwell in them, maybe instead
because the dark cleft at the nether end
reminded him too much of women.

Dog children, cat children, human, bird:
the broad bean, as I saw today,
even has umbilicals, as if
to signify that everything is loss, is child.
Can there be mind without suffering?
Can there be living without damage?
I just don't know. A famous Australian poet
once wrote a 'Broad Bean Sermon'. I

re-read it almost an hour ago, looking
for something that I can't quite name,
but no, all is abundance there, and populace.

Tonight I've prepared them, lightly charred,
with salt and lemon juice, olive oil,
cayenne pepper, parsley
and mint from under the laurel tree,
and eat them slowly, thinking.
Rich, succulent, piquant, they taste of waiting.

Report from Blue Mountains

I.

My *Echium*, exotic that it is,
has collapsed under the weight of its own blossoming.
This afternoon, while I tried to string it,
the sun slipped behind a bank of cloud
and the first fat drops of a heavy shower fell.
As I climbed the steps to the back veranda, the dog following,
I saw a tiny beetle on the handrail
hesitate and turn, as if deciding to make for home.
The rain, as I sat in the doorway, thundered on the roof, like
    wonder,
halting us all.

2.

It is spring in the mountains, uncertain spring.
One day it hails and the temperature drops,
the next it is windy and thirty degrees.
Plants bolt upward and then stop, as if thinking they have
    come too far.
The grass is thick and wild, full of dandelions, scotch thistle,
    rogue poppies, dock.
This morning I found myself longing for a country
where no-one understands me.
Tonight a large moth has been keeping me company,
dusting my shoulders with her yellow wings.

Lamplight

Lux, my fair falcon,
where are you now?
Tossed in some black gale again?
Buffetted by heart, by snow?

My nights' harrier harried,
time-hurt and hiding,
her bronze tuft whitened,
her slender spine made bow?

Or are you still riding
the high air somewhere,
your eye your mind's arrow,
scouring the fields below?

Ah, my love, my golden,
I don't need to be told.
You won't come to my wrist again;
this arm cannot hold.

'Windmill'

1.

What we call a
'windmill' is in fact a wind-
driven water-pump,
and what the
Dutch might call such
(if the Dutch
were speaking English) is
a wind-driven engine for the
milling of
grain into flour.

2.

A true
'windmill' if you
could find one would
grind the wind, but into
what flour, for what
bread?

3.

The rusty
blades of an old wind-
driven water-

pump as they
turn in the night
breeze
mill air into
sound and, further
down,
sadness, memory, the little
loaves of regret.

The Motherboard

Adrian, my next-door neighbour,
has asked me for a poem
and it seems the least that I can do,
so let this be its own explanation – how
my mother died just on forty-two years ago,
on May 24th,
and over and again, though
not every year,
has come back to wreak a kind of havoc
on that or the days around it
as if there were some unfinished
business she has with me
or wants me to finish with the world,
this year amongst the worst, starting
with a meeting missed and moving on
through a crashed computer, a broken-down lawnmower,
    our car
dying at 9 p.m. on Lapstone Hill
and finishing
as I tried to get to sleep at last
with a wind so wild that, as
I'd find on waking, it tore down the rotten
and ivy-covered pine
at the bottom of the yard
smashing a hole in our common fence
wide enough for a truck to drive through.

It's the motherboard, the technician tells me,
and as I mull that over, Saturday May 26th, after
a long sleep-in, making
coffee and looking out over the valley, the lawn-
mower back, the computer and the car to come
and most of the tree cut up and gone, congratulating
myself for coming through,
I hear a tapping I can't identify and,
listening more closely,
moving to the right, craning
for a view around the fern tree,
down there in the grey morning light, un-
bidden, emerged
from his own wild weather, settling
an old score with the world perhaps
and absorbed in the rhythm of its doing,
see Adrian
from next door, with a long
piece of two-by-four,
mending our fence.

Midsummer

Midsummer and a south-east wind
bringing autumn cold,

twelve days of rain
rotting the tomato plants,

battering the lettuces,
washing the seedlings away.

What else to do
but read poetry,

sleep winter-like sleep,
drink water straight from the sky?

Money Like Water

Money falls about us like rain.
It trickles along the gutters,
slickens the stairs and the balcony,
flows into the downpipe drain,
slips through our fingers,
gathers in pools the colour of sky.

Piped into our houses
we flush with money,
we wash with money,
we clean our cars with money,
we feed money to our children,
we ripen our fields with money.

People go to the desert to flee money
or form communes to keep it at bay,
but the air is thick with money,
the trees drip with money,
dig far enough into the soil
and the money will be there.

It leaks through our pockets,
drains from our wallets,
seeps from the things we've bought.
Its subtle acidity
riddles our conversation,
eats holes in our thought.

Stored injudiciously
money will evaporate.
Stored too tightly it will release
malignant vapours when exposed to light.
Accept money and you may never be at peace.
Refuse, and you may die from the want of it.

Old money and new money alike
can penetrate the soul.
Floorboards are rotted by money.
Foundations are undermined by money.
A house built on money
will never keep the ghosts away.

The rising tides of money
are making our streets impassable.
The melting glaciers of money
are deepening the sea.
The empty containers of our money
clog every waterway.

Venice is drowning in money.
Vanuatu is drowning in money.
They say that the human body
is ninety-three per cent money.
They say that we will choke on our own money.
They say there is no other way.

At Refuge

for Lynda S.

The day's heat, unrelenting,
trips the catch of evening, revealing
the rodents' empire, the roving
firmaments of moths.

The great
factory of the spiders
hums in stillness.
The black pond glazes with starlight.

How
not to be longing?
How not to write of the heart?

Morning, Station Street

Awake at seven after not enough sleep,
try again until eight-thirty,
then up, shave, shower, dress,
turn on the computer, greet and feed the dog,
check emails – twelve already – discard five,
answer four, set three aside (one
disappointment, two to be thought about)
then go out to speak with Paul
who's arrived to work on the roof; climb
up with him, discuss the job, come back down
to call the telephone company, spend ten
minutes on hold, leave a message, call
the bank to arrange a funds transfer; make
coffee, clean up last night's dishes, stare
out at the day awhile, thinking: the sky
a cloudless blue for once, light a lush
margarine yellow, four
sleek white cockatoos on the new fence
preening themselves, crests erect, waiting
their turn at the seed-bowl, the call
of a koel somewhere, and a whipbird, the yard
full of blossoming clover, the coffee
when I get to it
strong, dark, intense.

Silent Night

Christmas Eve, and the dogs are exchanging
season's greetings over the backblocks,
the smell of a barbeque over the fence
filling the air with sacrifice,
the ritual about to commence,
the festival of gluttony and slaughter,
cooks stuffing their turkeys,
children clustering about the Christmas tree
like ants at sugar water.

All day the lists and anxiety,
the rudeness at the checkouts,
the anger in the parking lots,
the loneliness in the shuttered houses,
the ragged nativities on the lawns,
police busy and the highways choked,
suicides preparing their Stilnox,
paramedics checking their stocks
of oxygen, adrenalin, morphine.

Christmas Eve, and the long-distance phone calls,
the Bloody Marys, the *Glühwein*, the priests
and the ministers sharpening their prayers, hosts
scraping and salting their grill-plates,
checking their bar fridge, their prawns on ice,
the Queen delivering her annual message,
pleading for peace and family,
regretting that her husband, in hospital for a stent,
won't be presiding over this year's hunt.

Christmas Eve, and all through the house
the tension, the expectation, the wonder.
Soon the children will be fed.
Soon they will be put to bed.
Soon the carols will begin
for a world redeemed of sin:
Silent night, crystal night …
Soon the tables will be set.
Soon the ovens will be lit.

'Unto us
a child is born,
unto us a Son is given',
and from the squalor of the feedlots,
the horror of the holding yards,
the abject terror of the abattoirs,
under mute, indifferent stars,
unthought, unvoiced, ungiven,
the cows, the sheep, the geese look on.

White Cockatoos

Gold-
crested Sultans of
the Real, white
cockatoos winch
the day into us,
crank it away.

*

White
cockatoos
litter the grass
like laundry
or so some
poet said.

*

At the edge
of the oval at twilight,
undoing the Council's
new-made lawn,
the white cockatoos
are like lilies on a wide dark pond.

*

White cockatoos
confound us;
they are animal,
they know
no matter how closely we watch them
our mind cannot see.

*

Could white cockatoos
know
that theirs is the colour of death?
A white cockatoo
crossing the sky at dusk
out-mourns the crow.

*

Wings
clipped, under duress,
a white cockatoo
will mimic the language of his oppressors.
In the language of the cockatoo
there are one hundred words for air.

*

A white cockatoo flying low at midday signals rain.
Swooping into the forest canopy,
weaving through the laneways of the pines,
pulling seeds
through the ankles of the grass,
they stitch us to the sky.

*

White cockatoos are raucous, larrikin,
no better word for a group of them but *gang*.
Feed them
and they will flock to you. Forget
and morning by morning
they will dismantle your house.

*

The memory
of white cockatoos
effaces us all. They know
the highways of the air.
Day after day
they lesson us. We fail and fail.

*

Creak
of boughs
in the frozen forest.
What is heavier,
the weight of a snowfall
or a hundred white cockatoos?

*

Arrayed on the telephone wires,
eyes
closed, motionless at sunset,
white cockatoos
are sleek
as white cockatoos.

*

The sound
of a flock
of white cockatoos
rising about one without
shrieking
is like a whisper from the second sky.

*

          Crown   rush
                Sultan   white   seed
branch   air   swoop
          without   sky
                flight lane   gang
larrikin   crest
            let   go

*

On the golf course, by the water-trap, one
coal-black
currawong, sulphur-
eyed, and fifty black-
eyed
white cockatoos.

Cock-crow

The mind doesn't always go to it
but the place is there;
the past, memory, regret:
they say it gets sharper every year.

Lying awake
at 4 a.m.,
trying to find its metres and its rhymes,
I hear the cocks crow a hundred times.

Black Dog

A whole
day goes by.
Where does it go?
And what is time anyway? Clouds
breaking up as they move westward, sun
warm on the back,
that black
dog from the feed store on Camp Street
coming at last to my hand.

Night Waking

Rain all night, hard rain, clearing the gutters, filling the tanks,
making a lake from the gully below. Waking
at 3 a.m. I could hear the wind
buffeting the house, soughing
in the maple and fir, the blown
water lashing the windows, clattering on the iron roof,
bringing the ocean over the Penrith plain,
and gale-borne cock-crows, dog-barks
thrown in and snatched away. After twenty minutes, up
for a pee, my own dog stretching,
coming to lick at my hand, my knee,
I returned to bed, felt
for your feet in the blankets, warm and dry, lay
in the grey dawn, thinking.

Who I Am

Who I am
no longer seems to matter
the way it once did

I am my father's son
but my father is dead

I am my mother's only born
but my mother is gone

I am my own child's father
and my child's mother
no longer speaks to me

I am a friend of my friends
but they have their own lives to attend

I am my new wife's husband
She is like daylight

Reading to the Sheep

Ark

Here at dusk the white cockatoos
swoop in to land on the grass, the saw-horse, the
unfinished fences.
Ark! Ark! Ark! they cry
as if they know something
we might not know.

Hidden Valley

At the top of the slope, by the water tank,
the two sheep are gazing
into the invisible

while three wild wood ducks
sit huddled
motionless by the pond
and a fourth swims.

The day began
hours ago.

Where have I been?

Accomplishment

There is Accomplishment
in washing-up
and cleaning the kitchen, Art
in stacking the dishes, Technique
and Experience in the prior rinsing, getting
the sequence right so that the water stays hot and
clear as long as possible, Order and Good
Governance in putting away
the bottles and jars, re-
cycling the scraps
from breakfast or last night's meal, and something else
in doing it all so quietly that one does not disturb the person
    still sleeping in the next room or the other
spirits of the house, thinking as they are this morning so
    attently
or the butcher bird watching from the balcony-rail, stilling
the soul to this Meniality, finding
the Joy in it.

Ram in the Rain

Such silence there was
before the rain
and then it came
and clattered on the fibreglass
the ram
went to shelter under the deck
a cockroach came out
to savour the ozone
the branches
that had been hanging low in the heat
stirred
and I sat
and stared into the darkness where it seemed
an absence waited
but then it stopped
and the ram came out
and I rubbed deep into his wool
hard against his ribs and spine
and he leant his weight
heavily against mine
and I breathed
almost easily again
knowing that there is no going.

Mort Street

For fifty years
wherever I've been
I've felt I've camped out in my life;
even this house, on this
land I love so dearly,
bought from a bankrupt council clerk,
shored against fire, against wind,
is like a tent on rolling ground.

From dawn until midnight, year's
start to end
we are travellers
whether we take to the road or not,
the hours of the day
like stations on a line we'll
never find our way back to – this
damp I've watched rising
almost a decade now, that
half-read book
I leant on the shelf there when
was it? October? last
year?

Reading to the Sheep

It is a cold afternoon in early winter and my wife
is reading to the sheep the first departmental seminar paper
from her doctoral thesis while unbeknownst to her
I watch through the kitchen window. She is wearing
her heavy winter jacket, and the sheep
in their thickening coats
are chewing on the already-stripped stalks of the rampant
    mint
and what is left of the autumn grass around the potato bed.
The thesis is on the grief of animals and she is reading
about the mourning of chickens for their mates,
about the grief of calves for their mothers, mothers for their
    stolen calves,
about huge elephants in the Kenyan dusk
turning over and over the bones of their dead,
she is reading about birds
placing branches over the bodies of their companions,
and about how, knowing that they did not know, the Lord
of some people or another – maybe it was ours –
sent crows to teach them due
reverence and rites for the departed,[xii]
she is reading about ants, carrying away
so carefully the bodies of their fellows,
she is reading about dogs
starving themselves after the loss of their loved ones,
about dolphins holding, at the surface of the water, their
    dying friends,
about macaque mothers carrying their infants
for months after the last breath has left them.

Now and again, when she pauses, lost
in the incipience of her own sorrow, perhaps,
or just asking for breath,
one or another of the two sheep comes to her
in the sad May twilight
and with the top of his head, where
the horns have not so long ago been sawn away,
nudges her hand
as if to comfort her,
or perhaps only to ask her to turn a page.

The light thickens, and a wind picks up. Ducks
settle about her, and the sheep
rest at her feet. Night
turns into day, then night, then day again.
Rain comes and goes. The seminar passes. Spring
turns into early summer, drifts on towards autumn.
The sheep rise, stretch, graze, return,
leaves pile around them and are blown
away by the winds of another winter.
Your hair
turns grey – look at it! – and a million lines
come to the backs of your hands.
You find this poem.
She is still reading.

Mountain Night

Mountain night, mist
among dark trunks
cutting visible distances

mind
going out into emptiness
feeling along ghost ridges
seeking the long plain

breathing
as the body breathes,
in deeply, out again

Orpheus

Orpheus Pumpkin, two-
week-old lamb,
is singing through the house
perhaps in search of his dead mother
whom he seems to think
speaks to him through the heating-vent.
His 2 a.m. bleatings
wander through our dreams;
his broad, horizontal ears and wide
astonished eyes
ambush the dawn.
Where he came from no one knows, some
chink in the heart perhaps, or
secret spring of night, or door
left open at the edge of thought,
his tiny hooves
a whisper in the evening grass,
his budding horns
barnacles in a rockpool
still turbulent with winter.

Birthday Poem

Wounds salved, heart straightened,
I take the years since I met you
as time given,
a decade I'd not have had otherwise.
If I've regrets
whose life is without them?
If I have debts let the creditors come.
The rain this morning
was like the first rain,
the sun in your eyes the first sun.

Humans at the Gate

Humans
at the gate,

rotund and briefcased,
pamphlets in hand,

wanting to tell us
about Christ our Saviour.

No point in asking
if they eat meat: lamb

sandwiches in the car, milky
tea in the thermos

yoghurt
for the acidophilus.

The Ornamental Cherry

I don't know if it is just
that sheep like eating the drying leaves
of the normally-out-of-reach
ornamental cherry,
for something in their bright-
orange fire perhaps,
or if instead it is the game they love, or the simple fact
that it is she who is feeding them
as one might give
manna back to the angels,
but every evening
for almost a week now
they have gathered there, in the autumn twilight,
waiting for my wife to come
with her soft, loving voice
and her strong arms,
to stand there with them
as the light goes
and reach up
into the golden boughs.

Driving Home

Sky
over the mountains
full of cloud caverns, huge
banks of darkness
massing to the west; by the gas
station on Albion Street
the traffic lights
glowing like emeralds; the dry
bones of the trees
as I open the gate
stirring at the forest edge, the cold
chain knocking against hardwood, nothing
itself tonight, mind
shut out of mind, the last
quarter of the waning moon
adrift over deepening flood.

Afterthought

You turn around,
go back upstairs,
but the room is almost empty,
someone is packing up the chairs.

'Forgotten something?', they ask,
and you say, 'No';
'Good night', they say,
and you say it too.

The Lambs

There's a telling congruence, it seems to me,
between certain tales from the Bible
concerning members of the species *Ovis aries* (sheep),
to wit lambs, rams, wethers, ewes – that
gruesome occasion, for example, when God
instructed Abraham to slaughter his son Isaac, as sacrifice
and proof of submission to the Divine Will, an order
which Abraham proceeded reluctantly to fulfil,
to be saved at the last moment when God, seeing
his willingness, proposed that he might substitute a ram; or
    that
second story, stranger still, though to Christians paramount,
unaware as it seems to me they'd have to be
of its curious anomaly, of God's preparedness
to sacrifice his own son, for the good, as it is said,
of all mankind – that son who, underlining that sense of
    sacrifice,
is so often referred to as the Lamb of God, the afore-
mentioned anomaly within which being that, if God
Himself is conducting a sacrifice, it must, unless
a supreme and eloquently troubling act
of vainglorious tautology,
have been to a further being whom He wished to placate
– that is, an unconscious and unintentional
admission on the part of the fabricators of such tales
of the nescience we invented God to deal with
in the first place. That, anyway, is how *I* deal
with the third and to me most troubling tale – that
of the Passover, and the awkward situation in which

God's Chosen People there find themselves, of having
to slaughter a lamb so that they might
mark their doors with blood, failure to do so
meaning that He would slaughter their first-born.
How to explain this? That in effect God says, *If you do not
slaughter a lamb then I will slaughter your
eldest child* – a correlate, as I have said, of tales 1 and 2,
not to mention a rather thuggish thing to do,
and a reminder, too, that 'sacrifice'
means *to* make sacred: it's all
to do with lambs, rams, ewes and wethers, it seems to me,
     not God,
a way to justify a choice of food
we know to be cruel beyond measure
but for which we nevertheless continue to hanker, though
not just that but – back to the tales – the curious way in
     which,
read carefully, we find them to admit it all: the
powerlessness of God, that darkness
within and about us, that
horror by means of which we
have chosen to survive, that
slaughter which we try to pretend
someone else is telling us to do; their
subtle displacements of their own assertions, so that (they
seem to whisper, to confess) lamb and ram, wether
and ewe
are made sacred, no whit less precious
or horrid to kill
than our own children.

Autumn Twilight

My old friend is gone
and there will be no more wine
drunk together under summer moons
and talk of the great poems
or the mastery of rhythm
or the elusive mysteries of being.

I am getting older myself
and should start to get used
to such precipitate departures.

But for now I'll take another glass alone
into the Autumn twilight
and go over again
some of the hard-won secrets
before the night comes
and the south wind blows them away.

Mushroom Season

A warm March day and I am drowsy
whether from age or some other cause
I just can't tell.
In the field outside the window
there is a sudden carpet of tiny yellow flowers,
the last thing you'd expect
given how low the sheep have
eaten the fodder down – but then
just yesterday, after the third day's rain,
the lawn out front
was scattered with small orange-topped mushrooms
and I remembered someone saying
that funghi can be vast organisms, trees
underground, and what we see
are only the blooms.
Just so, on tiny
spindle-stalks, and on the old stump
by the zucchini garden a bouquet
of scalloped wood-fungus, cream-
yellow, edged with brown, breath-
takingly beautiful in the fading light.

I could have let this all pass
and written nothing, but no, life
is a mushroom season;
we can never know
what will be of significance
to those who come after us: a flight
of birds, a pattern of weather, a spray of yellow
flowers in the short-cropped grass.

Each Other's Tongue

Coming out before bed
to watch the moonlight from the deck
I hear a pump still working
and going down to turn it off
suddenly can see the moon properly
its rays reaching from horizon to horizon
playing on a receding edge of cloud
and on the winter grass
and on the backs of the sheep
who to my surprise are still up, watching

One comes over
and I scratch his neck
deep under the thickening wool,
bending over
to catch his hot breath on my cheek
and together we murmur about moonlight,
for one brief moment
understanding each other's tongue

Notes

i   Hans Zinsser, *Rats, Lice and History*, 1935.

ii '*Les Chercheuses de Poux*' ('The Lice Pickers').

iii The Boria is a northerly wind, straight from the Alps. In Slovenian, *Burje*; often referred to elsewhere as the Bora.

iv 'An Absolutely Ordinary Rainbow'.

v As Pound relates at the end of Canto LXXXII: 'three solemn half notes / their white downy chests black-rimmed / on the middle wire'. The 'DTC' is the American Detention Training Centre in which Pound was held – initially in a wire cage – in 1945, awaiting extradition to the United States to face charges of treason.

vi As Canto LXXV, Pound reproduces a 1935 arrangement by Gerhart Münch (1907–1988) of *Le Chant des Oiseaux* by Clement Janequin (c.1483–1558).

vii Francis Webb, 'Five Days Old'.

viii See his *Birds of America*, 2nd ed, London, 1827–38. An online version is available at http://www.audubon.org/bird/BoA/BOA_index.html

ix For an interesting poetic treatment of the same phenomenon, see Robert Adamson's 'The Mullet Run', *Cross the Border*, Sydney, 1977.

x They slaughtered another 6000 a year later, at Majura, a few kilometres away, and have done so annually since. The official 'harvest' of kangaroos Australia-wide for 2009 was 3,985,531.

xi Bohumil Hrabal (1914–1997). His *Ostře sledované vlaky* (1965) was first published in English as *Close Watch on the Trains*, London, Cape Editions, 1968. In 1971 it was made into the film *Closely Watched Trains* by Jiří Menzel.

xii 'Then Allah sent a crow digging up the earth so that he might show him how he should cover the dead body of his brother.' – the Koran.

Acknowledgments

Poems from this collection have appeared in:

Arc (Canada): 'Ram in the Rain'
Australian Broadcasting Commission: 'Silent Night'
Australian Love Poems 2013: 'No Poem for Weeks Now',
    'Her Feet'
Best Australian Poems 2009: 'A Place on Earth', '*Ninox
    strenua*'
Best Australian Poems 2010: 'Rats, Lice and History'
Best Australian Poems 2012: 'Broad Bean Meditation'
Best Australian Poems 2013: 'Dust'
Best Australian Poems 2014: 'Silent Night'
Island: 'Who I Am'
Meanjin: 'A Place on Earth', 'Tinnitus', 'Spiders About
    the House', 'Looking for Andrei Gromyko', 'In the
    Kingdom of Shadows', 'Report from Blue Mountains',
    '"Windmill"' , 'Apricots', 'Another Page from the Book
    of Everything'
Melaleuca: 'Carmen 193'
Prosopopoeia (India): 'The Thick of It', 'Majesty'
Regime #5 (anthology): 'Mort Street', 'Driving Home',
    'Mountain Night'
Southerly: 'Mist', 'Silent Night'
TEXT: 'Plenitude'
The Canberra Times: 'Frcight'
The Dublin Review (Ireland): 'The River'
The Warwick Review (UK): 'Broad Bean Meditation'
Wet Ink: 'Poem'